BAPTISM
IN THE
HOLY SPIRIT

Other Whitaker House Titles
by Derek Prince

BAPTISM
IN THE
HOLY SPIRIT

DEREK PRINCE

⊞ *Whitaker House*

Unless otherwise indicated, all Scripture quotations are from the King James Version (KJV) of the Bible.

Scripture quotations marked (NAS) are from the *New American Standard Bible*, © 1960, 1962, 1968, 1971, 1973, 1975, 1977 by The Lockman Foundation. Used by permission.

BAPTISM IN THE HOLY SPIRIT

Derek Prince Ministries–International
P.O. Box 19501
Charlotte, NC 28219
www.dpmusa.org

ISBN: 0-88368-377-6
Printed in the United States of America
© 1995 by Derek Prince Ministries–International

Whitaker House
30 Hunt Valley Circle
New Kensington, PA 15068
www.whitakerhouse.com

---

5 6 7 8 9 10 11 12 13 14 / 11 10 09 08 07 06 05 04 03

Contents

A Study of
Prepositions

A Study of
Prepositions

*For by <u>one</u> Spirit are we all baptized
into one body, whether we be Jews or
Gentiles, whether we be bond or free;
and have been all made to drink
into one Spirit.*
—1 Corinthians 12:13

The baptism in the Holy Spirit is a topic which everyone is talking about. In the last few years, I have traveled and preached quite widely in three different continents. Everywhere I go, I find that the baptism is the topic of interest, discussion, and also, perhaps, controversy among Christians around the world.

Sometimes, Christians have the impression that speaking about spiritual things is largely a matter of emotion. Therefore, they believe that they will not have much need for their intelligence. This is a complete mistake.

Instead, we need to give very careful attention to the teaching of God's Word. Unless it is regarded with understanding, the information that you read here will be of little help to you.

The verse cited above needs a certain amount of clarification, since trouble has been created for many people due to the whims of translators. One prominent feature of the verse is repeated three times. This is the short but important word, *one*.

This verse cannot be properly appreciated unless it is realized that the apostle Paul's main emphasis was not on a doctrine but on the unity of the body of Christ. Apart from any individual and personal blessings that those of us who have had the blessing of being baptized in the Spirit may have received through the experience, we need continually to keep in the forefront of our minds that God's supreme purpose for bestowing it is the unity of the body of Christ. I do feel that many times we have not been centered in God's line of teaching and revelation because we have strayed from this foundational principle concerning the baptism in the Holy Spirit.

It so happens that I used to be a teacher of Greek at Cambridge University, and I've studied it since I was ten years old. So, in this respect, I dare to say that I know what I'm talking about. I do not doubt that some readers are also familiar with Greek and can turn to any literal translation or any commentary to check on the truth of the translation modification that I am about to make. However, I am not asking you to accept the minor modification because of my educational background. Rather, I am asking that you check into it for yourself.

I would say that 1 Corinthians 12:13 could be more accurately translated this way: *For in one Spirit were we all baptized into one body...and we were all given to drink of one Spirit* (author's translation). First, the preposition in the original Greek means "in" and not "by." That so many interpretations of this verse have been based on the word "by" is a minor tragedy.

With regard to the Greek verb *baptizo*, which means "to baptize," there are only two prepositions that ever follow it in the Greek New Testament. One is *en*, which means "in," and the other is *eis*, which means "into." No other prepositions ever follow it anywhere in the New Testament.

"In one Spirit," the verse says, *"were we all baptized."* This verb is in the past tense, not the perfect tense, and denotes a single event that took place at a certain moment in our past experience. It is not "we have been baptized," but *"we were baptized."*

Now, I do believe that, in order for us to appreciate the meaning of this verse fully, we need to consider certain parallel passages in the New Testament, particularly with regard to the use of the words *"baptized into,"* which is rather a strange phrase. You have probably met people who say, on the strength of this verse, that unless you have been baptized in the Holy Ghost, you are not a member of the body of Christ. I think this is a terrible thing to say. I respect the sincerity of those who say it, but I think it is a tremendous and basic error.

Therefore, before I go further, I want to try to clarify by reference to four other places in the New Testament where the phrase *"baptize into"* is used. After you look at the passages, I believe you will agree with me that in every case *"baptize into"* is used, the person baptized was already "in" what he was *"baptized into."*

The first place where it is used is in Matthew 3:11, *"I indeed baptize you with water unto repentance."* This is literally *"**into** repentance."* Does that mean the people whom John baptized had not previously repented or were not in a condition of repentance? Obviously not. This is clear if you look at the preceding verses:

> [7] *But when he saw many of the Pharisees and Sadducees come to his baptism, he said unto them, O generation of vipers, who hath warned you to flee from the wrath to come?*
> [8] *Bring forth therefore fruits meet for repentance.*   (Matthew 3:7–8)

In other words, John the Baptist was saying, "Demonstrate by your lives that you have repented, and then I'll consider baptizing you."

Therefore, it is perfectly clear that John baptized people whom he believed to have already repented. His baptism was outward evidence of his acknowledgment that they had repented, and if he had reason to believe that they had not repented, he would not have baptized them.

These are the words of Peter after the outpouring of the Holy Spirit on the Day of Pentecost in answer to the question of the convicted multitude:

> 37 *Now when they heard this, they were pricked in their heart, and said unto Peter and to the rest of the apostles, Men and brethren, what shall we do?*
> 38 *Then Peter said unto them, Repent, and be baptized every one of you in the name of Jesus Christ for the remission of sins, and ye shall receive the gift of the Holy Ghost.* (Acts 2:37–38)

Now, *"be baptized…for the remission of sins"* in the Greek is literally *"be baptized…into the remission of sins."* Does that mean their sins were not remitted before they were baptized? No, that would be contrary to the whole tenor of New Testament doctrine.

Their sins were remitted when they repented and put their faith in Jesus Christ. They were then baptized as an outward testimony that the apostles had met the conditions. Once again, they were already in the condition into which they were baptized.

Look at the following in Galatians:

24 *Wherefore the law was our schoolmaster to bring us unto Christ, that we might be justified by faith.*

25 *But after that faith is come, we are no longer under a schoolmaster.*

26 *For ye are all the children of God by faith in Christ Jesus.*

27 *For as many of you as have been baptized into Christ have put on Christ.*   (Galatians 3:24–27)

Notice again, the order is clear and decisive. In verse 26, we see that there is only one condition required to make a person a child of God—saving faith in Jesus Christ. Anything that teaches otherwise is a false doctrine.

In John 6:47, Jesus said, *"Verily, verily, I say unto you, He that believeth on me hath everlasting life."* This is more accurately translated as: *"He that believeth **into** me hath everlasting life."*

That is the doctrine for which Luther stood—justification by faith alone. Nothing but an active faith in Jesus Christ is required for a person to become a child of God. Then Paul goes on to say, *"as many of you as have been baptized **into** Christ have put on Christ."* Notice, they were already *in* Christ; then they were baptized *into* Christ as the acknowledgment that they were *in* Christ.

We read the following in the sixth chapter of Romans:

> [2] *God forbid. How shall we, that are dead to sin, live any longer therein?*
> [3] *Know ye not, that so many of us as were baptized into Jesus Christ were baptized into his death?*
> [4] *Therefore we are buried with him by baptism into death: that like as Christ was raised up from the dead by the glory of the Father, even so we also should walk in newness of life.*
>
> (Romans 6:2–4)

In this passage, we find the phrase *"baptized into"* used in reference to being *"baptized into"* the death of Jesus Christ. In this sense, Paul also spoke of baptism as a burial when he said, *"we are buried with him by baptism into death."*

Now, it is perfectly clear that we do not bury a person in order to make him dead. That would be a horrible thought! In fact, our burying a person constitutes our acknowledgment that that person is already dead. Thus, baptism *into* the death of Christ does not in itself produce the condition of being dead to sin in the person baptized; rather, it is the open acknowledgment that the condition has already been produced in that person through faith in the death and resurrection of Christ.

Thus, we have seen the same lesson four times. In each of the cases that we have considered, we have found that to baptize a person *into* any condition is to acknowledge publicly that the person is already *in* that all four cases, the context makes this absolutely plain.

Reading again from Paul's first letter to the church at Corinth, we find,

> [13] *For by one Spirit are we all baptized into one body, whether we be Jews or Gentiles, whether we be bond or free; and have been all made to drink into one Spirit.*
>
> (1 Corinthians 12:13)

We can now see the meaning of this passage in its true light. We were already *"in the body."* The baptism in the Holy Spirit acknowledges and makes public and effectual our membership in the body, of which we already have been a part. With the Holy Spirit baptism, we are all *"baptized into"* the oneness of the body. That is the purpose of the baptism in the Spirit. We were already *in* the body just as the people whom John baptized were already in repentance, just as the people baptized on the day of Pentecost were already in remission of sins, just as the people referred to in Galatians were already in Christ, and just as the people referred to in Romans were already dead to sin before they were buried by baptism into Christ's death.

Thus, we are already in the body of Christ. However, the baptism in the Holy Spirit is a supernatural seal that is given to each individual member by which Jesus Christ acknowledges the member as a part of His body.

Christ alone can confer this supernatural seal. Many different men baptized in water, but John said, *"This is the one who baptizes in the Holy Spirit"* (John 1:33 NASB). There is no one else in all Scripture to whom that privilege is given but to Jesus Christ, who thus acknowledges the membership of His body and sets the apostolic seal upon the believers who receive it.

Remember always that the ultimate purpose of the Holy Spirit baptism is the unity of Christ's body. It accomplishes this by making individual members of the body effective agents in bringing about unity, not division, in the body.

The Nature of the Experience

The Nature of the Experience

Now, let us consider the nature of this experience as described in the Scriptures and not as people sometimes speak about it in their testimonies.

When I was speaking in Copenhagen, a young man came up to me and said, "I have spoken with other tongues. It happened to me when I was alone. Do you think I have been baptized in the Holy Spirit?"

I said, "Yes, I do. I don't believe any other evidence is required if you have spoken in other tongues as the Holy Spirit gave you utterance."

"Well," he said, "whenever I hear other people speaking about this experience, they always talk about the wonderful emotions they had, the great joy and peace. I didn't feel any special emotion."

I replied, "You can't allow yourself to be led astray by people's testimonies. When the Bible speaks about the baptism in the Holy Spirit, in no case is there any direct reference to any kind of emotion whatever."

But, of course, it is a natural instinct in human beings, when we speak about an experience, to articulate the way it affected us. If it happened that our emotions were greatly stirred, that is the thing which we will highlight. However, it is *not* what the Bible emphasizes. You may check for yourself that there is no specific reference to emotion in the various places where the baptism in the Holy Spirit is written of and described.

Don't jump to a wrong conclusion, however. I am not arguing against emotion because emotion is part of the total human make-up. If a person's emotions are not converted, that person is not fully converted. I certainly believe that our emotions should be converted. They should form part of our total Christian experience. But, this is not an absolute with reference to the baptism in the Holy Spirit.

What does the Bible say about this? I believe the Bible uses two word pictures or figures. First of all, we read of *baptism*. In the New Testament, this word is used in connection with the Holy Ghost seven times, which is quite a large number. The other word that is also used by Paul is *drinking*. I believe that if we put these two together, we will form a comprehensive picture from the Scriptures of this experience.

Baptism

Baptism in an immersion, but this immersion comes from above. I do not want to be controversial, but while I was at Cambridge recently, I spent a day in various libraries researching the history of the word *baptize*. I traced it from the fifth century before Christ down to the second century of the Christian era. Its definition has never changed. It has always meant "to immerse."

We are talking about a baptism not of water but of the Holy Ghost, a coming down of God's Spirit from above over the believer, enveloping him in heaven's atmosphere. This is one aspect of the experience. We read in Acts,

> [2] *And suddenly there came a sound from heaven as of a rushing mighty wind, and it filled all the house where they were sitting.*
>
> (Acts 2:2)

The whole atmosphere around these believers was filled. They were immersed from above in the supernatural power and presence of God.

Now, I suppose there might be somebody reading this who would say to me, "Well, Mr. Prince, the book of Acts is merely historical. You have no right to preach doctrine from it."

On the other hand, however, the apostle Paul did not agree with that because he said,

> [16] *All scripture is given by inspiration of God, and is profitable for doctrine, for reproof, for correction, for instruction in righteousness.*   (2 Timothy 3:16)

Note what the order is in this verse. First, it says, *"Scripture...is profitable for doctrine."* Then it mentions that the Scriptures are profitable for reproof, correction, and instruction in righteousness. Therefore, since the book of Acts is part of Scripture, it is profitable for doctrine.

The Bible presents doctrines in two ways: as statements or commands, and as descriptions of experiences or events. When we combine the two, event and statement meet. We then have a clear picture of what the Bible speaks about because we have all of the information.

This is analogous to a jigsaw puzzle that you have put together, but one piece is missing. You can say, "Well, it should be green at the top and blue at the bottom, and it must stick out at this corner and go in at that corner." When you find the piece, it fits perfectly, and you click it in place. So it is with the baptism in the Holy Spirit: doctrine, experience, and the events described in the book of Acts all unite, and when it agrees from every angle, you know you've got it.

Let's look at the following in Acts:

¹⁴ *When the apostles which were at Jerusalem heard that Samaria had received the word of God, they sent unto them Peter and John:*
¹⁵ *Who, when they were come down, prayed for them, that they might receive the Holy Ghost:*
¹⁶ *(For as yet he was fallen upon none of them: only they were baptized in the name of the Lord Jesus.)*
¹⁷ *Then laid they their hands on them, and they received the Holy Ghost.* (Acts 8:14–17)

You notice the phrase, *"He was fallen upon none of them."* The receiving of the Holy Ghost coincided with the Holy Ghost falling upon them from above. Then, in the tenth chapter of Acts (I am assuming that people are familiar with the background of these events), we read:

> ⁴⁴ *While Peter yet spake these words, the Holy Ghost fell on all them which heard the word.*
> ⁴⁵ *And they of the circumcision which believed were astonished, as many as came with Peter, because that on the Gentiles also was poured out the gift of the Holy Ghost.*
> ⁴⁶ *For they heard them speak with tongues, and magnify God.*
>
> (Acts 10:44–46)

Notice that the Holy Spirit *"fell on them"* and *"was poured out"* on them. These phrases describe an immersion coming down from above. The Scripture is very consistent in the descriptive terms used.

Peter spoke about this to his colleagues in Jerusalem who had called him to account for his unorthodox behavior in going and preaching to the Gentiles. In modern language, he told them, "Well, what could I do? While I was speaking, the Holy Ghost fell on them as on us at the beginning. Who was I to resist God? He gave them the same gift that he poured out on us."

So, the whole thing is tied together: the baptism, the falling, the receiving, and the gift. They are simply different ways of describing one and the same experience.

A similar passage is located in Acts.

⁵ *When they heard this, they* [the disciples at Ephesus] *were baptized in the name of the Lord Jesus.*
⁶ *And when Paul had laid his hands upon them, the Holy Ghost came on them; and they spake with tongues, and prophesied.*

(Acts 19:5–6)

Notice the phrase *"came on them"* used in this Scripture. You can find the same picture described elsewhere, for I have not exhausted the references. However, I have sought to justify this as one primary aspect of the experience. The baptism is a supernatural coming down of the Holy Ghost over the believer, immersing him not in water but in the *shekinah* glory of God's presence. Whether it is visible or invisible is not the important question.

Drinking

The baptism is not merely something that comes down over us. It is also something that we receive into us. Paul says in 1 Corinthians 12:13 that we, *"have been all made to drink into one Spirit."* This ties in exactly with the words of Jesus in John's gospel:

> [37] *In the last day, that great day of the feast, Jesus stood and cried, saying, If any man thirst, let him come unto me, and drink.*
> [38] *He that believeth on me, as the scripture hath said, out of his belly*

shall flow rivers of living water.
[39] *(But this spake he of the Spirit, which they that believe on him should receive: for the Holy Ghost was not yet given; because that Jesus was not yet glorified.)*

(John 7:37–39)

This Scripture makes it plain. Jesus is referring to the gift of the Holy Ghost for the one who believes, and He compares the receiving of it to the act of drinking. He says, *"If any man thirst,"* which means, "if any man has a longing in his heart." He then says, *"let him come unto me, and drink,"* which is saying, "let him receive *into* him."

At that point, a marvelous miracle takes place as the thirsty person becomes rivers of living water. Instead of not having enough for himself, he becomes a channel of supply to many. Relating to others is one of the purposes of the baptism in the Holy Spirit. Maybe you have enough to get you to heaven, but you do not have enough for a needy world. You need the rivers that will flow out of your life.

When I served as a missionary in East Africa, I met many different kinds of people: Africans who had no education and no background, educated Africans, Hindu Asians, Asians who were Moslems, and the white people who in many cases regarded themselves as slightly superior to the others. When interacting with all of these people, I said as Paul did in 2 Corinthians 2:16, "*Who is sufficient for these things?*" Who can deal with the almost naked tribesman or the European in his palatial home? How can we truly meet with people? God reminded me of John 7:38, "*out of his belly shall flow* [not **a** river of living water, but] *rivers of living water.*" These rivers are enough for everybody. That's faith and experience.

The baptism is also perfectly logical. I actually wrote my fellowship dissertation on logic, and since I was converted, I have always rejoiced in the Bible because I find it the most logical book in the world. Its logic is flawless. As far as I am concerned, I have never found an error or a fault in it.

Matthew 12:34 says, "...*out of the abundance of the heart the mouth speaketh*." When the heart is so full that it can no longer hold its contents, where does it overflow? Through the mouth.

The baptism in the Holy Spirit is a supernatural infilling, and it is a supernatural overflow. How do you know when the vessel is full? It begins to overflow. I cannot see inside your heart or your spirit, and you cannot see inside mine. But, when I hear the overflow, I know it has been filled, and it is clear, logical, scriptural, and practical. If it is not practical, it is not scriptural!

Today, literally thousands of people are being baptized in the Holy Ghost just as I have described, and there are far more outside of the Pentecostal movement than inside it. For instance, I lived in Seattle, Washington, on the northwest coast of the United States for nine months. There are about forty Pentecostal churches in Seattle and one Episcopal mission church.

Do you know what an Episcopalian is? He is an Anglican that has strayed across the border of Canada into the United States. I had to discover that as I did not know what I was dealing with. I have been in that Episcopal mission church two or three times as a speaker, and actually, if I had not been told it was Episcopalian, I certainly would not have guessed because the atmosphere was, to say the least, distinctly lively.

The rector began by playing some Negro spirituals on his guitar. When the people praised the Lord, they all had their hands up in the air. There were very few inhibitions. When I talked to one of the ladies who worked in that mission, she conservatively estimated that two thousand people had been baptized in the Holy Spirit in this church during the previous three years.

I question whether two thousand people have been baptized in the Holy Spirit in all forty of the Pentecostal churches in that same time. This is not said to criticize anybody, but to emphasize my point that you can't always know people from their denominational labels.

Warnings

Warnings

Now, in view of all we have discussed, I want to throw a little cold water on you at this stage. I do not recommend that you seek the baptism in the Holy Spirit or any other spiritual experience unless you are deadly earnest with God. Otherwise, you should stay out of it because your condemnation will be all the greater, and your problems will also be all the greater. Holy Spirit baptism is not an exciting picnic organized by the Sunday school department. We put ourselves in extreme danger if we do not approach it in the right way and if we do not rightly relate it to other things in our spiritual experience.

With humility, I want to let you know that I have experienced the baptism and lived in it for well over forty years. In that time, I have seen the wreckage that comes about from the failure to relate this thing rightly to the rest of the Christian life, experience, and testimony. Let me briefly give you a few words of warning.

Baptism Is Not Forced

First of all, the Holy Spirit is not a dictator. He is our Comforter and our Teacher. He does not *make* you do things. The person who disturbs a meeting and then says, "I couldn't help it; the Holy Ghost made me do it," has a false picture of the Holy Spirit because He is *not* a dictator. If a spirit comes into your life and makes you do things, you have the wrong spirit.

You will not get any more from the Holy Ghost than you are willing to yield to Him. When some people receive the baptism in the Holy Spirit, they get very little noticeable benefit from it because they are not thereafter willing to be guided, counseled, directed, and controlled by the Holy Spirit. He does *not* force anyone against his will. The baptism demands a life of continual submission and waiting upon God. Somebody has said, "It is much easier to get filled with the Spirit than it is to stay filled with the Spirit." There is a lot of truth in that.

Baptism Is Not a Substitute

Secondly, the baptism in the Holy Spirit is not a substitute for any other provision of God. God has not given us any one experience that will do everything.

For instance, we read about the Christian armor in the sixth chapter of Ephesians. If you put all six pieces of armor on, you are covered from the crown of your head to the soles of your feet. If, however, you omit one of them, you are no longer fully protected. Suppose you forget the helmet, but you have the shield, the boots, the sword, the girdle, and the breastplate. Most of your body is covered, but your head is open to the enemy's attack. The thought-life of many Christians is not covered for this reason. They suffer head wounds and lose the power to manipulate the sword and the shield. They have only five pieces when they should have had six.

Here is another example. Some people say, "Well, brother, I've got love. I don't need the gifts." Experience has taught me to question how much love the people who speak like that really have. I would say love is shown mainly in action and not by assertion. Even so, the reasoning is unscriptural because the Bible says that we should have both. Love is not a substitute for the gifts of the Spirit, and the gifts of the Spirit are not a substitute for love.

First Corinthians 12:31 says, "*But covet earnestly the best gifts: and yet show I unto you a more excellent way.*" In a sense, the coveting of the best gifts is a condition of being shown the more excellent way, especially if you read the verse as it should be translated. *"Covet earnestly the best gifts, and I will show unto you a yet more excellent way,"* is a more accurate translation. First Corinthians 14:1 says, *"Follow after charity, **and** desire spiritual gifts."* This does not say "or desire spiritual gifts." You are not invited to take your choice. You are commanded to pursue both, and if you do not, you are not obeying the Word of God.

An Unfamiliar Realm

The baptism in the Holy Spirit is a spiritual experience, a supernatural experience. In many cases, it is the first supernatural experience that many Christians have ever had. As such, it ushers them into a new realm, and often, they are not at home in that realm.

Among other things, it is a realm of spiritual conflict that most of them never knew before they were baptized in the Holy Spirit. Let me give you a little example from the ministry of Jesus. Look at the following:

> [9] *And it came to pass in those days, that Jesus came from Nazareth of Galilee, and was baptized of John in Jordan.*
> [10] *And straightway coming up out of the water, he saw the heavens opened, and the Spirit like a dove descending upon him:*
> [11] *And there came a voice from heaven, saying, Thou art my beloved Son, in whom I am well pleased.*
> [12] *And immediately the Spirit driveth him into the wilderness.*
> [13] *And he was there in the wilderness forty days, tempted of Satan; and was with the wild beasts; and the angels ministered unto him.*
>
> (Mark 1:9–13)

This is the incident in which Jesus was anointed for His ministry. The Holy Spirit came down on him and thereafter abode upon Him.

Notice the next thing that happened as a direct consequence of this experience: "*And immediately the Spirit driveth him into the wilderness. And he was there in the wilderness forty days, tempted of Satan.*" That is not what humans would expect, but that is spiritual reality. The same kind of thing can happen in your life when you are baptized in the Holy Spirit. You enter into a new spiritual realm in which Satan and the demonic become much more real. Many new avenues into your mind and into your spirit are opened which were not open before. This is not a picnic; it is a reality.

I want you to observe one fact: Jesus overcame Satan, and He did so with one weapon, the written Word of God.

> [4] *But he answered and said, It is written, Man shall not live by bread alone, but by every word that proceedeth out of the mouth of God.*
> [5] *Then the devil taketh him up into the holy city, and setteth him on a pinnacle of the temple,*
> [6] *And saith unto him, If thou be the Son of God, cast thyself down: for it is written, He shall give his angels charge concerning thee: and in their hands they shall bear thee up, lest at any time thou dash thy foot against a stone.*

⁷ Jesus said unto him, It is written again, Thou shalt not tempt the Lord thy God.

⁸ Again, the devil taketh him up into an exceeding high mountain, and showeth him all the kingdoms of the world, and the glory of them;

⁹ And saith unto him, All these things will I give thee, if thou wilt fall down and worship me.

¹⁰ Then saith Jesus unto him, Get thee hence, Satan: for it is written, Thou shalt worship the Lord thy God, and him only shalt thou serve.

(Matthew 4:4–10)

Three times Jesus said, "*It is written.*" No one needs to know the written Word of God more than a person who has just been baptized in the Holy Spirit. You are in desperate need to study your Bible and to know it. Remember that even Satan can quote Scripture, and you have to be able to overcome him not only by being able to quote it better than he does but, more importantly, to be able to choose and wield the right Scripture because you know and understand the Word of God.

The baptism in the Holy Spirit must be united with the Word of God. Otherwise, it is very dangerous. Ephesians 6:17 says, *"Take...the sword of the Spirit, which is the word of God."* Notice that the sword of the Holy Spirit is the Word of God, and it is your responsibility to take it. If you take it, the Spirit will wield it through you, but if you do not take it, the Spirit has nothing to use. Oh, the problems that can arise when you are in that defenseless situation!

Finally, let me add this: being baptized in the Holy Spirit is no substitute for *obeying* the Word of God.

The Purposes of
the Experience

The Purposes of the Experience

I have been negative in order to be positive, if I may put it that way. There are a number of important purposes that the baptism in the Holy Spirit is intended by God to accomplish in the life of the believer. How much it will accomplish depends on the believer, however.

Gateway to the Supernatural

The following passage contains a great promise if you read it with discernment:

> *⁴ For it is impossible for those who were once enlightened, and have tasted of the heavenly gift, and were made partakers of the Holy Ghost,*
> *⁵ and have tasted the good word of God, and the powers of the age to come.* (Hebrews 6:4–5)

The *"partakers of the Holy Ghost"* have tasted the powers of the world to come. They have been brought into contact with a power that belongs to the next age, but it is available to them in this age. In this way, the baptism in the Holy Spirit is intended to be the gateway into the supernatural. It is not a goal; it is a gateway. It is intended by God that thereafter the Spirit-baptized believer should walk in the supernatural. In fact, if I may put it this way, the supernatural should become natural.

If you take the book of Acts as a picture of the Christian church, you will see a supernatural description as you read it. If you are intellectually honest, I offer this as a challenge to you: find one chapter out of the twenty-eight in Acts which would be left untouched if all references to the supernatural were removed. My answer is that not one of them, not one, would be left intact.

We cannot refer to New Testament Christianity without including the supernatural. At the very least, we can talk about it, but we cannot truly experience it.

I love Acts 19:11 in particular, which says, *"And God wrought special miracles by the hands of Paul."* Do you know what I like? I like the word *special.* In the original Greek, it means the kind of miracles that do not happen every day. In other words, miracles were an everyday occurrence in the early church, but these were something extraordinary. Even the early church turned around to pay attention to these.

Again, let me say that we can theorize all we want to about the New Testament church, but we cannot experience it without the supernatural. Be honest.

For Witnessing

> [8] *But ye shall receive power, after that the Holy Ghost is come upon you: and ye shall be witnesses unto me...* (Acts 1:8)

The baptism in the Holy Spirit is intended to clothe us with supernatural power from on high so that we can be witnesses. Notice that witnesses are *unto* Jesus Christ. They are not unto a doctrine and not primarily unto an experience but unto Jesus Himself. Many of us in the Pentecostal movement have gone astray through becoming witnesses to a denomination, a church, or an experience. However, the true purpose is to witness to Jesus Christ. You will find the people who use it that way are tremendously successful.

For Prayer

This experience also produces a revolution in a Christian's prayer life. Let's look at Romans for a moment:

> [26] *Likewise the Spirit also helpeth our infirmities: for we know not what we should pray for as we ought: but the Spirit itself maketh intercession for us with groanings which cannot be uttered.*
> [27] *And he that searcheth the hearts knoweth what is the mind of the Spirit, because he maketh intercession for the saints according to the will of God.* (Romans 8:26–27)

Notice that we all have an infirmity. It is not a sickness, but it is a natural weakness of the flesh. We do not know how to pray as we ought to pray. Not one person exists who does.

I can say (and I trust I will not be misunderstood) that I have often heard dear brothers in student prayer meetings. I have listened to those sincere, educated young men who studiously pour over their words as they tell almighty God what He ought to be doing.

That is not really prayer. God does not need to be told what to do. Groping with the intellect to find exactly the right thing to tell God to do next is not

New Testament prayer; rather, in New Testament prayer, the believer becomes a temple in which a Person comes in and conducts a prayer meeting. That Person is the Holy Ghost. We simply become an instrument.

Tibetan priests have what they call a prayer wheel. While they are saying their prayers, they are turning the prayer wheel, and the wheel is supposedly doing the praying. When you are baptized in the Holy Ghost, you become a kind of prayer wheel. The Holy Spirit turns you around and prays through you. It is marvelous.

A lady who is known to many was born and raised in the Roman Catholic religion in Ireland. She came to London, where she was saved and baptized in the Holy Spirit. At the time, she worked as a maid in a hotel in London, and she shared a room with another Irish Catholic girl.

One day, the other girl said to her, "I want to ask you something. I hope you don't mind, but every night after you have gone to bed and you seem to be asleep, I hear you talking some foreign language. What is that language?" That young lady got to know for the first time that every night after her body was asleep, the Holy Ghost was praying through her.

Read what the Scripture says about the bride of Christ: *"I sleep, but my heart waketh..."* (Song of Songs 5:2). That's a spiritual reality. Concerning the fire on the altar of the tabernacle in the Old Testament, it also says, *"The fire shall ever be burning upon the altar; it shall never go out"* (Leviticus 6:13). That is a picture of the Holy Ghost on the altar of the believer's heart, a fire burning night and day.

Let me show you two other Scriptures. Ephesians 6:18 says, *"Praying always with all prayer and supplication in the Spirit."* Notice that is says praying *always* in the Spirit. You cannot always pray in your understanding. You cannot always pray in your physical body. But, when the Holy Spirit is there, He doesn't quit.

The same thought is also found in 1 Thessalonians, chapter five, where it says, *"Pray without ceasing"* (v. 17), and *"Quench not the Spirit"* (v. 19). These two are related. You can quench the Spirit. You can put the fire out, but it is not God's will. The baptism in the Holy Spirit kindles a fire. Remember what Paul said to Timothy: "Fan it up again; make it blaze; don't neglect the gift that is in you." (See 1 Timothy 4:14.)

With that same word, I challenge anybody that does not have this supernatural experience, because it is an impossibility for him to live up to the New Testament standard of prayer. That is what I mean when I say New Testament Christianity is supernatural; it cannot be otherwise.

For Teaching

[13] *Howbeit when he, the Spirit of truth, is come, he will guide you into all truth: for he shall not speak of himself; but whatsoever he shall hear, that shall he speak:*

and he will show you things to come. (John 16:13)

[26] *But the Comforter, which is the Holy Ghost, whom the Father will send in my name, he shall teach you all things, and bring all things to your remembrance, whatsoever I have said unto you.*

(John 14:26)

The Holy Spirit is the great Teacher of the Scriptures. Jesus Christ promised that when the Spirit of truth came, He would lead us into all truth, teach us, and bring to us a remembrance of all Jesus has said.

The Holy Spirit is also the great Revealer of Jesus Christ. The apostle John said, *"He shall glorify me"* (John 16:14). These two functions go together because Jesus is the living Word and the Bible is the written Word. The Holy Spirit is the author of the written Word, and He is the one who comes in to be the Interpreter of the Word.

In 1941, while serving as a soldier in the British Army, I was invited by another soldier to attend a Pentecostal service. I had no idea that it was a Pentecostal service, and I did not know then that Pentecostal people existed. I had never heard of them. Had I known anything about them, I might have hesitated to go.

At that time, I had just spent seven years at Cambridge studying philosophy, and I held a fellowship at King's College, Cambridge. If anybody ever went to a religious service with a critical attitude, I was that person. I said to myself, "I'll see whether this preacher really knows what he's talking about." The preacher did not know this, but that was my viewpoint. After I had listened to him for a while, I formed two clear and definite conclusions. The first conclusion was that the preacher *did* know what he was talking about, and the second was that I *did not*.

One thing impressed me. As he talked about David, talked about Saul, talked about Samuel, and talked about a whole host of other biblical characters, his relationship to them was such that I thought he had met them that morning. I thought to myself, "Where did he ever get to know these people like that?"

Years ago, while I was in school, I had a fairly accurate memory and was good at the Bible. I always scored over ninety percent in that rather monotonous morning session that was imposed upon us. However, that had been about fourteen years before this incident. When I was baptized in the Holy Ghost (which happened in an army barracks room shortly after I first heard that Pentecostal preacher), every one of those Bible stories that I had studied as a child became as clear and vivid to me as if I had read them the previous day. Who did that? The Holy Ghost. He is the Teacher.

We need human teachers, too, so don't be a fanatic. The Holy Spirit can teach you through another believer. I add that because I have met people who think that they do not need to be taught when they have the Holy Ghost. However, He is the Teacher and Revealer of

Jesus Christ. He shows you where Jesus is more clearly than anything else.

Do you know where Christ is? He is seated at the right hand of almighty God, and *"all power is given* [Him] *in heaven and in earth"* (Matthew 28:18). When the Holy Spirit fell on the Day of Pentecost, it was like a personal letter from the Lord for those disciples cloistered away in that Upper Room. To them the letter read, "I have arrived; I'm here. You saw me go; now you know where I am."

Shortly after that, Peter stood up and told those unbelieving, Christ-rejecting Jews,

> [33] *Therefore being by the right hand of God exalted, and having received of the Father the promise of the Holy Ghost, he hath shed forth this, which ye now see and hear.* (Acts 2:33)

Peter knew where Jesus was in a new way. Who made that so clear to Him? The Holy Spirit did.

To Exalt Christ

My first wife, Lydia, was a staunch Lutheran in the Danish state church. Many years prior to her death, she was baptized in the Holy Ghost one night in her room. Nobody had pressured her, influenced her, or taught her about it. It was a gift directly from heaven. The change in her life was so dramatic that she did not know what to do, so she went to an elderly, respected pastor in the Lutheran church in Copenhagen. She had heard he was more spiritual than many of the other pastors.

Lydia said, "I wonder whether you can help me. I have a problem."

The pastor was concerned about this young lady who came with a problem. "What is it?" he asked.

"Well," she said, "something has happened to me, but I'm not sure what."

"Can you describe it?" he asked.

"Now, when I pray," she replied, "I feel I'm facing Jesus."

That Lutheran pastor more than thirty years ago replied, "Sister, you must have been baptized in the Holy Ghost."

That's what the baptism in the Holy Spirit is for—to exalt Jesus.

For Guidance

Another aspect of the Spirit's ministry is that of guidance and warning.

> [13] *Howbeit when he, the Spirit of truth, is come, he will guide you into all truth: for he shall not speak of himself; but whatsoever he shall hear, that shall he speak: and he will show you things to come.* (John 16:13)

We need that. We need supernatural warning and direction to survive in the world we live in today. If we live merely in the natural, we will go wrong many times.

Let me remind you what Jesus said in Luke 17:26: "*And as it was in the days of Noe, so shall it be also in the days of the Son of man.*" We think about the sin and the iniquity that abounded in the days of Noah, and we say it is like that today. But remember, there was something else in Noah's day. By faith, he was warned by God of things that were not yet seen, and he moved with fear as he prepared the ark. Noah had a supernatural revelation of what was coming on the earth. He knew the steps to take, and he knew the way to safety. In the same way, you and I who are living in these atomic days need to have contact with heaven in a very real and personal way.

Jesus said, *"He shall not speak of himself; but whatsoever he shall hear, that shall he speak"* (John 16:13). We are ushered into the councils of heaven when we are baptized in the Holy Ghost and listen to the still, small voice of the Spirit. I can testify personally about this, having traveled many thousands of miles and having been in many lonely and dangerous places. I want to acknowledge the supernatural direction and revelation of the Holy Spirit that has revealed to me many times what was to come next. His guidance has enabled me to take the right action. We definitely need this today.

For Health

Now, let me show you a passage from 2 Corinthians:

> ¹⁰ *Always bearing about in the body the dying of the Lord Jesus, that the life also of Jesus might be made manifest in our body.*
> ¹¹ *For we which live are alway delivered unto death for Jesus' sake, that the life also of Jesus might be made manifest in our mortal flesh.* (2 Corinthians 4:10–11)

Notice that the life of Jesus is to be made manifest in our mortal flesh. Not merely are we to have this invisible, unseen life, but it is to be *visibly manifested* in our bodies. What is the life of Jesus? It is resurrection life, victorious life, powerful life. It is God's will that it should be manifest in our mortal flesh.

What room does that leave for the works of the devil in our bodies? Notice the word *"manifest"* is used twice in those two verses. In truth, this is divine healing, yet it is more. It is divine health and eternal resurrection life that is now penetrating, operating, and manifesting itself in our mortal bodies.

Who is the administrator of this life? Turn for a moment to Romans 8:10: *"And if Christ be in you, the body is dead because of sin; but the Spirit is life because of righteousness."* Isn't that wonderful?

The night I got saved, I didn't know anything about the doctrine of salvation. After all, I had been educated at Eton and King's, so what would I know about salvation? I say that jokingly, but it is a sad thing. However, it is a fact that up to the age of twenty-five, I had never heard the Gospel preached. I had never met a person who could testify to a personal experience of being born again.

People talk about darkest Africa, but I have never met an African that was in grosser spiritual darkness than I was after seven years at Cambridge. At that time, I was a habitual, inveterate blasphemer, and I was also an extremely heavy drinker. I did not know what salvation was, but a moment came when I knew that I had met people who had something I did not have. I reasoned that God could not be unfair, so if He gave it to them, He must give it to me.

I asked Him for it and got it somewhere after midnight in an army barracks room. The next day, I no longer blasphemed. When I went to the pub to buy a drink, my legs would not walk inside. It was astonishing how they would not go through that door! I was under new management. I did not even want a drink, and it was only habit that took me to that place.

What broke the power of blasphemy and drink like that? Christ had come in, and the old body was dead. A dead body does not lust for drink. A dead body does not blaspheme. A new life had come in. What life? *"The Spirit is life because of righteousness"* (Romans 8:10). Being justified by faith in Jesus Christ, we have access to a new life. The Spirit comes in and gives us *"life because of righteousness."*

Continuing to read in Romans, we find,

> [11] *But if the Spirit of him that raised up Jesus from the dead dwell in you, he that raised up Christ from the dead shall also quicken your mortal bodies by his Spirit that dwelleth in you.*
>
> (Romans 8:11)

That is the Holy Spirit, the Administrator of the resurrection life of Jesus, imparting it to our mortal bodies.

Not coincidentally, almost everywhere that people are baptized in the Holy Ghost, they begin to pray for the sick. I can scarcely think of an exception. I know there are some who are not baptized in the Holy Ghost, yet they have seen prayer for healing in the Scriptures and faithfully practice it. God honors their prayers. God did it for the disciples, too, even before the

Day of Pentecost. We read that the disciples went out during the earthly ministry of Jesus and anointed many of the sick with oil. They also cast out demons. So, God will honor those who pray for the sick even if they have not received the baptism.

Nevertheless, it is a fact that wherever the Holy Spirit has come in as the Administrator of divine life from Jesus Christ, almost instantly, He illuminates the eyes of God's people to see that this life is not merely for the inward man but for the outward man as well. Almost inevitably, you will find that this happens.

For Unity

Finally, I return to my initial text.

[13] *For by one Spirit are we all baptized into one body, whether we be Jews or Gentiles, whether we be bond or free; and have been all made to drink into one Spirit.*

(1 Corinthians 12:13)

Remember this: the ultimate purpose of God in baptizing believers in the Holy Spirit is to unite them and not to separate them.

Somebody complained about a certain church in the United States where the minister had been baptized in the Holy Spirit. Some of the congregation had gone along with him while others had not. The person said, "The trouble with this experience is that it is dividing the church." To this dubious statement, another minister, whom I know personally, responded with this excellent answer: "That's remarkable, because in the early church it had exactly the opposite effect. When the Jews heard the Gentiles speak with other tongues, it was the only thing that united Jews and Gentiles in one church and one body. Nothing else would have done it."

Likewise, the only thing that will bring Baptists, Plymouth Brethren, Assemblies of God members, Anglicans, Lutherans, Presbyterians, and many other denominations together in large numbers—embracing one another, throwing their arms up in the air, spending hours praising God—is the baptism in the Holy Ghost.

Let me tell you of an incident that made a deep impression on me. I was speaking at a convention of the Full Gospel Businessmen in Spokane, Washington. It was held in a big hotel where several hundred people were present. I was teaching the afternoon Bible study, especially warning those in attendance about the dangers of fooling around with Pentecost. When I had come to the end of my message, I did not know what to do since they had no specified program.

(Can you say "Praise God"? Many Pentecostal people have programmed the Holy Ghost out of most Pentecostal churches. Did you know that? They do not allow room for the Holy Spirit to move, and they would be shocked if He did. They would have to stop doing something, which would upset them.)

Having no set program is what I like about the Full Gospel Businessmen.

They may begin at *Z* and end at *A*. You never know what will happen. I have been the main speaker at some of their breakfasts and have not even begun to speak until half-past eleven in the morning.

Not knowing what else to do, I just stood there and was silent. Soon a lady began to sing in an unknown tongue. I would describe it as a kind of Gregorian chant. It so happened that the brother who was with me on the platform was a choir leader and quite an expert in music. When she had finished singing, he said, "That was a very complicated melody." We waited a little while, and a young man began to sing in English. He gave the interpretation of that song which was in an unknown tongue, singing in exactly the same melody. The words that he sang also fit the melody. The man beside me said, "He kept the melody perfectly." In the course of the day, this happened twice.

The interesting part of this whole story is that I did something that we do not often do at these conventions.

We rarely ask others what their denomination affiliations are, since we are not concerned about particular labels. However, because it seemed to tie in so perfectly with the subject at hand, I made some inquiries about the denominational alliances of these two people. I discovered that the lady was a Lutheran and the young man was an Episcopalian. However, we were all one in Jesus Christ in the unity of the Holy Ghost.

Today, the church of Jesus Christ faces two alternatives. On the one hand, we have *union,* and on the other, we have *unity.* I will not go as far as to say that these two are mutually exclusive. However, I close with the thought that man can make union, but only the Holy Ghost can make unity.

About the Author

About the Author

Derek Prince (1915–2003) was born in Bangalore, India, into a British military family. He was educated as a scholar of classical languages (Greek, Latin, Hebrew, and Aramaic) at Eton College and Cambridge University in England and later at Hebrew University, Israel. As a student, he was a philosopher and self-proclaimed atheist. He held a fellowship in Ancient and Modern Philosophy at King's College, Cambridge.

While in the British Medical Corps during World War II, Prince began to study the Bible as a philosophical work. Converted through a powerful encounter with Jesus Christ, he was baptized in the Holy Spirit a few days later. This life-changing experience altered the whole course of his life, which he thereafter devoted to studying and teaching the Bible as the Word of God.

Discharged from the army in Jerusalem in 1945, he married Lydia Christensen, founder of a children's home there. Upon their marriage, he immediately became father to Lydia's eight adopted daughters—six Jewish, one Palestinian Arab, one English. Together the family saw the rebirth of the state of Israel in 1948. In the late 1950s, Derek and Lydia adopted another daughter while he was serving as principal of a college in Kenya.

In 1963 the Princes immigrated to the United States and pastored a church in Seattle. Stirred by the tragedy of John F. Kennedy's assassination, he began to teach Americans how to intercede for their nation. In 1973 he became one of the founders of Intercessors for America. His book *Shaping History through Prayer and Fasting* has awakened Christians around the world to their responsibility to pray for their governments. Many consider underground translations of the book as instrumental in the fall of communist regimes in the USSR, East Germany, and Czechoslovakia.

Lydia Prince died in 1975, and in 1978 Derek married Ruth Baker (a single mother to three adopted children). He met his second wife, like his first, while she was serving the Lord in Jerusalem. Ruth died in December 1998 in Jerusalem where they had lived since 1981.

Until a few years before his own death in 2003 at the age of 88, Prince persisted in the ministry God had called him to as he traveled the world, imparting God's revealed truth, praying for the sick and afflicted, and sharing his prophetic insights into world events in the light of Scripture. He wrote over 45 books, which have been translated in over 60 languages and distributed worldwide. He pioneered teaching on such groundbreaking themes as generational curses, the biblical significance of Israel, and demonology.

Derek Prince Ministries, with its international headquarters in Charlotte, North Carolina, continues to distribute his teachings and to train missionaries, church leaders, and congregations through its worldwide branch offices. His radio program, *Keys to Successful Living,* began in 1979 and has been translated into over a dozen languages. Estimates are that Derek Prince's clear, non-denominational, non-sectarian teaching of the Bible has reached more than half the globe.

Internationally recognized as a Bible scholar and spiritual patriarch, Derek Prince taught and ministered on six continents for over seven decades. In 2002 he said, "It is my desire—and I believe the Lord's desire—that this ministry continue the work, which God began through me over sixty years ago, until Jesus returns."

Shaping History through Prayer and Fasting
Derek Prince

The times we are living in are scary, to say the least, yet what we are facing isn't new. History is replete with violent episodes of unimaginable carnage and terror. And what did people do about them? The only thing they could do—they prayed! Discover with Derek Prince how your prayers can make a difference. You can learn to touch the heart of God through effective fasting and prayer—prayer that can change the world!

ISBN: 0-88368-773-9 • Trade • 192 pages

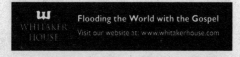

Flooding the World with the Gospel
Visit our website at: www.whitakerhouse.com

Derek Prince on Experiencing God's Power
Derek Prince

Derek Prince shows how to receive God's promises regarding healing, fasting, marriage, spiritual warfare, finances, prayer, the Holy Spirit, and much more. In this unique guide, you will find answers to some of life's toughest issues, and you will discover how to achieve powerful results in your spiritual quest. A valuable addition for your library, this anthology is a collection of nine of Derek Prince's best-sellers!

ISBN: 0-88368-551-5 • Trade • 528 pages